THE SEATED WOMAN

ALSO BY CLÉMENCE DUMAS-CÔTÉ

L'alphabet du don, 2017

Glu, 2022

ALSO TRANSLATED BY E. S. TAILLON

Scenes from the Underground, 2022

THE SEATED WOMAN

POEMS

CLÉMENCE DUMAS-CÔTÉ

TRANSLATED BY E. S. TAILLON

ARACHNIDE

First published as *La femme assise* in 2019 by Éditions Les Herbes rouges
First published in English in 2025 by House of Anansi Press Inc.
houseofanansi.com

House of Anansi Press is committed to protecting our natural environment. This book is made of material from well-managed FSC®-certified forests, recycled materials, and other controlled sources.

House of Anansi Press is a Global Certified Accessible™ (GCA by Benetech) publisher. The ebook version of this book meets stringent accessibility standards and is available to readers with print disabilities.

29 28 27 26 25 1 2 3 4 5

Library and Archives Canada Cataloguing in Publication
Title: The seated woman : poems / Clémence Dumas-Côté ; translated by E.S. Taillon.
Other titles: Femme assise. English
Names: Dumas-Côté, Clémence, 1986- author. | Taillon, E. S., translator.
Description: Translation of: La femme assise. | In English, translated from the French.
Identifiers: Canadiana (print) 20240431561 | Canadiana (ebook) 2024043692X |
ISBN 9781487013295 (softcover) | ISBN 9781487013301 (EPUB)
Subjects: LCGFT: Poetry.
Classification: LCC PS8607.U44319 F4613 2025 | DDC C841/.6—dc23

Cover design: Greg Tabor
Cover image: Jens Magnusson / Ikon Images / SCIENCE PHOTO LIBRARY
Book design and typesetting: Lucia Kim

House of Anansi Press is grateful for the privilege to work on and create from the Traditional Territory of many Nations, including the Anishinabeg, the Wendat, and the Haudenosaunee, as well as the Treaty Lands of the Mississaugas of the Credit.

Canada Council for the Arts
Conseil des Arts du Canada

ONTARIO ARTS COUNCIL
CONSEIL DES ARTS DE L'ONTARIO
an Ontario government agency
un organisme du gouvernement de l'Ontario

With the participation of the Government of Canada
Avec la participation du gouvernement du Canada | Canada

We acknowledge for their financial support of our publishing program the Canada Council for the Arts, the Ontario Arts Council, and the Government of Canada.

Printed and bound in Canada

FSC www.fsc.org
MIX
Paper | Supporting responsible forestry
FSC® C103567

For Zola, for Cléo, for Glass Eye
For Félix

Quand je suis assise, je pense, j'écris, je rature ;
quand je me lève, je tremble, toussote, m'emballe
parce qu'entre ma voix écrite et ma voix réelle,
il y a le dragon de soi.

CAROLE DAVID
Manuel de poétique à l'intention
des jeunes filles

When I'm sitting, I think, I write, I scratch out;
when I stand up, I shake, clear my throat, get carried away
because between my written voice and my real voice,
there's the dragon of the self.

CAROLE DAVID
Guide to Poetry for Young Girls

CONTENTS

THE SEATED WOMAN

CHARACTERS

THE POEMS

THE SEATED WOMAN

We are the poems,
we watch over your total eclipses.

You are a seated woman
identical to the others,
you keep watch and you write.

You shape the interval
in which we might sink our fingers
to open the storm of the century.

We bring the metronome,
we will play opposite you—
you handle the score.

VOCAL STARVATION

THE SEATED WOMAN

I say star
first reddening star
at the end of its savings.

THE POEMS

You have to intuit a mic here.
We live in the science fiction
under your dress, a chaos
that you would call devastation.

THE POEMS

It's okay, little war,
you don't have to punctuate the Bible
just listen to the radio:
"I am alive
I belong to reality for mama."

If we ask you,
you will reply calmly:
"The living room first was named boudoir
and sometimes, pact."

THE SEATED WOMAN
It's okay, murderers
with your spray of sound
I wander.

THE POEMS
You nibble on our carbon, its possibility
you offered us a file on your archaeology
in it, we read the following:

THE SEATED WOMAN, *whispering.*
"Here is my light after the excavation."

THE POEMS

Your spectre convulses
a drum solo in the eye,
it lets out just three or four words.

You hate this whole secret
now, go all-out, a book of poems.

THE POEMS

We stash away some carrion crows
(relics) because objects break
we make love to you, slow like the plague
when your pen presses hard on our risk
and drafts us, baby document.

We wish to breathe in your most beautiful phantom landscape.

THE POEMS

You don't know that we kidnapped your diaphragm

under siege, you were disappearing
we could no longer trust in your stillness.

The evenings' provisions are ready
you will act as Archangel before the explosion.

THE SEATED WOMAN

Will I make it through?

THE POEMS

Lying under a map,
you'll hold for the hum
you'll clap your hands together
you'll have had a stomach ache for five years.

SALT OF SATURN

THE POEMS

Come, burn a planet.

(If you sweep out your Christmas
blues, the runoff,
the faded wedding,
in stereo we will wait:
invisible poinsettias in the middle of the suburbs.)

THE POEMS

We resuscitate—our disjointed carcasses
(salt and air) fill your throat.
You retreat inward, wings closed.

On the ground: residue of a couplet, origami.

THE SEATED WOMAN

My feeding is clumsy.
    Fumbling with her voice.
"On the ground: a femicide.
On the ground: my irises
and a pile of chewed wrists."

THE POEMS, *repeating themselves; in canon.*
Would you twist our fists,
our streak, our blessing,
our favourite waste of time?

You planned yourself a crime
you disguised yourself as a cart
and you blew out the candles
along the road patiently.
We are signalling in wide strokes—
do you read us?

THE SEATED WOMAN

If I found you as gentle as a yoking
maybe with a swiftness, a trampoline rhythm
smooth as butter,
my soul would emerge.

Instead you send me space facts
and launch your boots at the ceiling.

I am much too much, too young to
but I'm starting to deflate.

THE SEATED WOMAN, *putting on a mask; having a cigarette.*
Let's try some cheery apparel,
let's warp ourselves, fur or felt.
Backlit: someone resembles you.
"Do you have a light?"

THE POEMS
See our castle dug into the back seat
on a mission, imagine your day, close by.
There are CF-18s filling the sky:
as soon as they're cut, their talons regrow
our graffiti lines your throat.

THE POEMS

This is your face
we set it on fire
carry its remains
ponytail over heels

in the basement, immaterial,
you play.

THE SEATED WOMAN

It's haunted; get back here.

I came under a theatre poster,
my whole mouth with your hands.

NIGHT TEACHING

THE POEMS

At your place, there was
no skin, just
a wall of methane
on which to watch the end.

We pull back from the shot.

THE POEMS

You fell asleep on the tiles,
a translucent peacock loomed,
your sex opened and let out
a very blue, very high flame.

You wore a split veil, that morning.

THE POEMS

The baby's gloves
archive your tart sadness,
we tear their fabric
so you suspect our presence.
We climb, you feel it.
You saw the forensic shadows,
The composition reveals them—

A drywall screw pierces your skull.

THE SEATED WOMAN

I can't help what my back does
when you go help yourselves in the room of entrails.

As long as I run in circles,
as long as I show up, strips of cloth joined
between my breasts, you will drag along a twelve-year-old voyage.

THE POEMS

This room used to behave like a bathroom.